DEVELOPING LEADERS IN A GROWING CHURCH

EMMANUEL O. Uthman

Developing Leaders in a Growing Church

BIBLE QUOTATIONS FROM KJV

E-mail: euthman2001@yahoo.com

Table of Contents

Leader makes people do, what they don't like to do and make them enjoy doing it.

CHAPTER ONE

WHO IS A LEADER?

A leader is a person who leads others, giving them direction and showing the way for others to follow.

"Behold, I have given him for a witness to the people, a leader and commander to the people." Isa.55: 4.

A leader must have a commanding influence. Leader makes people do, what they don't like to do and make them enjoy doing it. The leader leaves nothing to chance, his daily fine tunes his leadership skills. Having carefully thought out his plan of action, the leader deliberately exerts special influence. His vision is deliberate (Even when he receives a divine call he responds). His choice of group is deliberate. His selection of goals is deliberate his assessment of the real needs of the group is deliberate. Leadership is the discipline of deliberately exerting special influence within a group to move it toward goals of beneficial permanence that fulfill the groups real needs. Leadership is a discipline. It is hard work. It takes effort and concentration, it takes staying power. Leadership is deliberate.

1. Leading is the ability to cause people to take effective action towards the leader's vision or the group common goals.
2. Looking through Webster Dictionary leadership is defined in this way: ***"It is the ability to lead."***

To be a leader you must be able to lead, you are not a leader by virtue of your position. You are a leader by virtue of your performance.

Those who occupy position without the ability to lead are just

there temporary, until those with leadership ability comes in and take over, because people follow leadership good or bad.
To be a leader, you may not even have a little, if you have the leadership ability and skills, without little you will still be the most significant leader.
Webster say that the verb ***"To Lead"*** means "To Show the way, to conduct, to guide, to direct the course of another by going before or along with.

A. A leader is one who does two things. **First**, he knows where is going. He has a clear-cut objective.

Second, he is able to persuade others to go along with him. And it is the balance of these two objectives and motivations that determines your success as a leader. Many people have great ability to stir the imaginations of people and gather a following, but they really don't know where they are going, such leaders will lead people down a blind alley. Some other know precisely where they are going and they are going to the right place but they cannot persuade others to go along with them, because they lack the ability to lead. To succeed as a leader you must know where you are going, you must be able to make people to follow you.

"Be ye followers of me, even as I also am of Christ." 1 Cor.11: 1

B. One major strand of leadership is conceptual. By that I mean, a leader is a person deeply infected with a concept, an idea, a cause or a vision. Nehemiah had a vision of rebuilding the walls of Jerusalem, he moved the people towards that direction, despite oppositions.

"Then said I unto them, ye see the distress that we are in, how Jerusalem lieth waste, and the gates thereof are burned with fire: come and let us build up the wall of Jerusalem that we be no more a reproach ... and they

said, let us rise up and build. So they strengthened their hands for this good work." Neh.2: 17-18.

They re-built the wall, because one men had the vision and he successfully moved the people towards the actualization of his vision. That is leadership.

C. The second aspect, there is a relational element. A good leader needs to have interest in the people. He must love the people the love must be genuine, real, practical, sacrificial and beneficial. People don't care how much you know, they are concern to know how much you care.

Don't only think of what to get from the people, think of what you can give to the people. Their welfare must be your concern. What do they stand to gain by associating with you?

"I am the good Shepherd: The good shepherd giveth his life for the Sheep: The hireling fleeth: Because he is an hireling, and careth not for the Sheep." John 10: 11, 13.

Ask yourself as leader, do you love the people, enough that you can die for them. Do the people know that you love them? That you can do everything for them. Even hurt yourself because of your followers.

TWO QUESTIONS THAT IDENTIFY A LEADER

What is it that really keeps you awake at night? In another word, what is it that really drives you? (Write it down).

Where are you men? A leader his know by those who are following. If you cannot point to a core of men and women into whose lives you are building you are not leader. Look at the example of Paul in 1 Thess.2: 1-20.

"For ye are our glory and joy." Vs.20 He had a goal and he was people oriented.

Like Ezra make up your mind to study the Bible for yourself and then teach others.

CHAPTER TWO

WHAT YOU MUST KNOW IN OTHER TO LEAD

How can you become a man who knows where is going?

A) You must develop deep personal convictions. These convictions are the ideals that make a leader.

To do that – you need to consistently study the Bible.

"Study to shew yourself approved unto God, a work men that needeth not be ashamed, rightly dividing the word of truth" 2 Timothy 2: 15. Like Ezra make up your mind to study the Bible for yourself and then teach others.

"For Ezra had prepared his heart to seek the law of the LORD, and to do it, and to teach in Israel statutes and judgements" Ezra 7: 10. Don't change the order, study the word – apply it to your life or situation and then teach others, what you have practice personally.

To be an effective and efficient leader, you need consistent guidance.

"Trust in the LORD with all thine heart; and lean not unto thine own understanding. In all thy ways acknowledge him and he shall direct thy paths" Prov.3: 5-6.

To get guidance you must wait on the Lord, you must depend on Him, trust Him for divine wisdom. God is able to make you stand – Rom.14: 4.

A. You need to develop personal schedule.

Discipline involves control of self. It is a lifelong process; you need to allow the spirit of God to control every area of your life. Don't copy another person's schedule. Be yourself, master yourself and your schedule.

B. To be an effective leader, you must sub-ordinate all of your life under your goal.

You must learn to say ***"No,"*** to the things that are not beneficial to your goals. You must know how to take decision and choose your priorities.

C. You need a willingness to make some hard-nosed decisions.

Remember when we say, ***"Here is a man of accomplishment,"*** we are really saying, ***"Here stood a man who can make a decision of the will."*** He once said, ***"I will do that, I will be that, I will go there."***

D. You need to embrace a sense of mission, and of destiny.

The problems you will face are not as important as to the way you see yourself. How do you mirror yourself?" ***And there we saw the giants, the sons of Anak, which come of the giants: And we were in our own sight as grasshoppers, and so we were in their sight" Num.13: 33.***

Don't under-estimate yourself, to over-estimate the strength of your enemy. If God be for you, no man shall be able to stand against you.

E. To be able to lead people, you must learn to live with tension, the realization that you have never arrived.

You are pursuing a flying goals, because as you progress, your goals progress.

"I press toward the mark for the prize of the high calling of God in Christ Jesus. Let us therefore, as many as be perfect, be thus minded: and if in anything ye be otherwise minded, God shall reveal even this unto you" Philippians 3: 3-15.

In the spiritual realm problems are essential to progress. Therefore, you must see problem as potentials for growth. Adversity means advancement, in the spiritual realm.

F. You must work smarter, not harder.

You must learn to distinguish between activity and accomplishment.

CHAPTER THREE

MARKS OF A MATURE LEADER

The Bible is clear to those who are aspiring to be leaders in the Church of Christ. What are the qualities they must possess?

"This is a true saying, if a man desire the office of a bishop, he desireth a good work. A bishop then must be blameless, the husband of one wife, vigilant, sober of good behavior, given to hospitality, apt to teach; Not given to wine, no striker, not greedy of filthy lucre, but patient, not a brawler, not covetous, one ruleth well his own house, having his children in subjection with all gravity; (For if a man know not how to rule his own house, how shall he take care of the church of God?) Not a novice, lest being lifted up with condemnation of the devil" 1 Tim.3: 1-6. "Wherefore, brethren, look ye out among you seven men of honest report, full of the Holy Ghost and wisdom, whom we may appoint over this business" Acts 6: 3.

Those who want to be leaders in the church today must possess godly virtues.

STAYING POWER: A leader must be resilient, but equally tough. He must have the ability to staying; he should not give up the responsibilities that had been apportioned to him. He must not abandon his role in the face of opposition, dare to be like Nehemiah.

"And I said, should such a man as I flee? And who is there, that, being as I am, would go into the temple to save his life? I will not go in" Neh.6: 11.

Nehemiah refused the counsel for him to abandon his responsibility for the safety of his life.

"And I sent messengers unto them, saying, I am doing a great work, so that I cannot come down: Why should the work cease, whilst I leave it, and come down to you" Neh.6: 3.

Because Nehemiah knows what he was supposed to be doing, he did not allowed opposition, critic, blackmail and threat to his life to stop him. The key to leadership is endurance.

VIRILE PRIVATE LIFE: If you must be strong in public, you have to be strong in your private life. You have to grow inside before you can grow outside. You must build up yourself to be able to do an effective service.
To be able to do that you need the word of the Lord to Elijah, "Go hide yourself" 1 Kgs.17: 3. we all need a quiet place, where we resort for strength and courage. You must prepare for effective action by clear thinking. And the best thinking is done in solicitude. Find a quiet time and place to seat and re-lax yourself for prayer, meditation, thinking and writing. Don't be too busy not observe a quiet time

"And the apostles gathered themselves together unto Jesus, and told him all things, both what they had done, and what they had taught. And he said unto them, come ye yourselves apart into a desert place, and rest a while: For there were many coming and going, and they had no leisure so much as to eat. And they departed into a desert place by ship privately" Mark 6: 30-32.

We all need a place of retreat, every, busy man need a time of resting and vacation.

SELF MASTERY: Every leader must control every area of his life.

A. **TIME:** You must be good time manager, you must watch your schedule, are you the one filling up your schedule or others are filling it up for you.

"Walk in wisdom toward them that are without, redeeming them time" Col.4: 5.

Your time is your life, when you are wasting your time; you are wasting your life. Time is money, when you waste your time; you wasting what can give you valuable amount of money.

Don't be idle, idleness leads to poverty. The idle man is the devil's workshop. Save yourself from laziness, be ready to do your own business ***"Not slothful in business; fervent in spirit; serving the Lord," Rom.12: 11.***

B. MONEY: *Money is valuable you must know, how to manage the money that will come your way.*

You need to be faithful steward of money, not wasting money, but spending it wisely for the purpose they are intended to spend it for, don't spend above your income don't buy the thing you cannot pay for; don't for the habit of borrowing, until you have lost your reputation.

"Owe no man anything, but to love one another: For he that loveth another hath fulfilled the law."

"His Lord said unto him, well done, good and faithful servant; thou hast been faithful over a few things enter thou into the joy of thy Lord" Matt.25: 23.

C. TEMPRAMENT: *A leader most controls his emotions and temperament, in other to remain in his position.*

When a leader fails to control his temper, he will lose respect in the sight of his follower,

"He that is slow to anger is better than the mighty; and he that ruleth his spirit than he that taketh a city" Pro.16: 32.

Every area of your life must be watch, your appetite, feelings, emotions, lust, discouragement etc. Every one of them must be brought under the sovereign control of the Holy Spirit.

"This I say then, walk in the Spirit, and ye shall not fulfill the lust of the flesh" Gal.5: 16.

D. **MODEL:** The fourth characteristic of a mature leader is that he is a consistent example.

Great leaders where good followers, before you can be a great leader you must have follow a leader, who you're modeling your life after, to whom you have been submissive. You must have serve that leader, you need to have passed through a tutorage, to become a mature leader.

Joshua served Moses before God called him and used him; he was Moses servant before he became the servant of the Lord. Elisha was the servant of Elijah before he became the prophet of God to Israel, he served Elijah faithfully, followed him all the way till the power of the God of Elijah came upon his life. There was transference of anointing from the leader to the followers. You remember the twelve apostles of the lamb, the followed the Lord all the way, when there was vacuum as a result of the sin of Judas Iscariot, they looked for a men who had been following them all the way ***"Wherefore of these men which have companied with us all the time that the Lord Jesus went in and out among us..." Acts 1: 21.*** Paul was a model to Timothy, Titus and others, as a leader you are also supposed to be a model to your followers. Even when you don't know it, there is an eye watching you. Paul told Timothy. ***"Let no man despise thy youth; but be thou an example of the believers, in word, in conversation, in charity, in Spirit, in faith, in purity" 1 Tim.4: 12.***

E. **RESISTANCE:** You must have strong resistance quality.

People are bound to oppose you, criticize you, speak false things about you, and speak unkind words to you. You must resist those oppositions; have a deaf hear to such oppositions. Plug your ears to such unkind criticism. David was criticize by his eldest brother heard when he spoke unto the men; and Eli-ab's anger was kindle against David, and he said, why comest thou down hither? And with whom hast thou left those few sheep in the wilderness?

I know thy pride, and the naughtiness of thine heart; for thou art come down that thou mightest see the battle. Look David's respond.

"And David said, what have I now done? Is there not a cause?" 1

Sam.17: 28-29.

I love David's bold respond; a leader must focus his eyes on his vision and goals, not on the noise or the volume of oppositions. Turn a deaf ear, look forward, step out; those who are against you never see what you are seeing. They will come back to praise you. You see the level of oppositions that Nehemiah faced, he waved them off to accomplish his goals.

F. **SERVANTHOOD:** The way up is the way down.

You must offer yourself to serve before you can become a great leader, you must be ready to serve the people before you can expect them to follow you. Are you ready to be the servant of God and the people of God, the greater your service, the larger your followers Jesus said He came to serve; we must be willing to serve. The greatest is the servant of all. ***"And there was a strife among them, which of them should be accounted the greatest. And he said unto them, the kings of the Gentiles exercise authority over them; and they that exercise authority upon them are called benefactors. But ye shall not be so; but he that is greatest among you; let him be as the younger; and he that is chief, as he that doth serve. For whether is greater, he that setteth at meat, or he that serveth. Is not he that sitteth" Lk.22: 24-27.***

You must beware of power without submission, absolute power destroys absolutely, if your motive in leadership is to get power to rule others, you must repent, because that is an in ordinate ambition. Be ready to submit yourself to God and the people of God.

"Submitting yourselves one to another in the fear of God" Eph.5: 21.

G. **CONFIDENCE:** A leader must possess a high confidence quotient.

Many great dreams are dead because the dreamer lacked confidence to declare it. Whenever we are unsure of ourselves, our project, our hopes, we usually remain silent.

If you are sure of your vision, you must be bold to declare it; if you know what God wants you to do be ready to go all out for it.

You will disappoint God and your followers if you quit because of difficulties.
"The righteous are bold as a lion."
To be able to work for God you need to be bold and of courage. That was what God told Joshua.
"Be strong and a good courage ... only be thou strong and very courageous ..." Josh.1: 6, 7.
No venture no success. You must declare. Like Paul.
"I can do all things through Christ which strengtheneth me" Phi.4: 13. Replaced self-confidence with Christ confidence. When you are standing with God the stumbling block with becomes stepping-stone. Dare to be bold, like Daniel, who stood his ground, and became master of the lions. Be bold, be strong for the Lord your God is with you, you are not alone.

H. **POSITIVE ATTITUDE:** A leader must have the right attitude, the problem and the challenges that will come your way is not as important as the attitude you show to any given situation.

Your attitude can make you or ruin you. The way act or react to situation. ***"For as he thinketh in his heart, so is he ..." Prov.23: 7.***
When you think wrongly, you will act wrongly. When positively you will act or react positively.
God is within you, don't under-estimate yourself. You can do all that God had called you to do.
Don't dwell on what you cannot do, there are many things you can do, what you cannot do today, you will discover you may capable of doing them later in life.

I. **PERCEPTION:** A true leader is a perceptive person.

He is forward looking, yet he's discerning of the present. He is future – oriented but he is presently involved.
" ... And a wise man's heart discerneth both time and judgement. Because to every purpose there is time and judgement, therefore the misery of man is great upon him. For he knoweth not that which shall be for who can tell him when it shall be?" Eccl.8: 5-7.

J. **TEACHABILE:** A leader must be teachable.

We must be ready to learn from the Lord and those God has given the grace to teach us. The leader must not poise as if he know it all. Teach-able a person's capacity for growth. "But grow in the grace and in knowledge of our Lord and Savior" 2 Peter 3: 18. This means to continue to grow ... make it a habit to grow in your knowledge of Christ.

Study your Bible, read good books, attend seminars, take advantage of any opportunity that comes your way for your development and effectiveness in leadership and ministering. ***"Study to shew thyself approved unto God, a workmen that needeth not to be ashamed, rightly dividing the word of truth" 2 Tim.2: 15.***

K. **FAITH:** A leader believes God for His specialty.

A leader chosen by God must be a man of faith. ***"But without faith it is impossible to please him; for he that cometh to God must believe that he is, and that he is a rewarder of them that diligently seek him" Heb.11: 6.***

You cannot walk with God without faith. You must have faith in what God had entrusted into your hand, you must hold in faith no matter the situation. You must have faith God who sent you, without faith in God, you will surely fail, ***"... Have faith in God" Mk.11: 22.*** As a leader you must have faith in your people.

Let your followers know that you have faith in them. Tell them you believe in God and in their faithfulness.

Faith will change your situations and circumstance. When you have faith, you will be ready to take the risk and get the result. Your faith can move mountain. You need unshakable faith in God to do something that count now and for eternity.

L. **PRAYER:** The leader must be a man of prayer.

Our Lord Jesus Christ, our leader and commander, the captain of our faith was a man of prayer. We must pray as if all depend on prayer. Prayer is the art of communion with God. If we must succeed, we must pray.

You must devise a prayer schedule. Discipline yourself to pray. Pray in public and in your private life pray for everything you have to do.

"And he spake a parable unto them to this end, that men ought always to pray, and not to faint" Lk.18: 1.

Paul even sought the prayer of other Christian,

In prayer, and watch in the same with thanksgiving: Withal praying also for us, that God would open unto us a door of utterance to speak the mystery of "Continue Christ for which I am also in bonds" Col.4: 2-3.

Leaders give people direction.

CHAPTER FOUR

THE NEED FOR LEADERS

The church like any other community needs leaders to channel her programs and defend her interest. Leadership is very important in any organization or society. The need for leaders cannot be over-emphasized. When there is no leader, there will be confusion and chaos. The leaders of any community are to maintain order and discipline within the community. Our church cannot survive without a leader who will give the people a sense of direction. The children Sunday school department of any denomination cannot survive without capable and committed leaders. Often times, we discover the need for leaders and hurriedly appoint somebody who apparently is a novice to the task of leadership.

Leaders are needed because without them the group will be open to attack, and nobody will alert the other or gather the people to defend themselves.

Let us look at a case in Judges 18: 1-2, 7-10: We understand the people live carelessly because there was no king. Their enemies found it easy to capture them and take them for slaves.

In Judges 17: 6, we are made to understand that because there was no king in Israel every man did as he like. That is dangerous for any community. Can you imagine a church without a pastor or any known leader; everybody comes to church to do something without anyone to put them to order; can you imagine the confusion it will cause?

That was the case with children of Israel – no leader, no guide, no judge, everybody doing things, as he felt fit to do it.

God doesn't want a situation where there is no leader. He could tolerate bad leadership until good leadership can be found. Look at the case of King Saul, (1 Samuel 15: 10-11; 16: 1).
God rejected him from being a king, but did not drive him away from the throne, until He found a king after his heart. Even when David was anointed as king, Saul was still left on the throne till the time he was killed.
God is not a co fusionist. We must learn a lesson from God's dealing with Saul, so that we are not being tolerated by God but appreciated by Him.

CHAPTER FIVE

WHY LEADERS ARE NEEDED

"And the Lord said unto Moses, Gather unto me seventy men of the elders of Israel, whom thou knowest to be the elders of the people, and officers over them; and bring them unto the tabernacle of the congregation, that they may stand there with thee. [17] And I will come down and talk with thee there: and I will take of the spirit which is upon thee, and will put it upon them; and they shall bear the burden of the people with thee, that thou bear it not thyself alone. [18] And say thou unto the people, Sanctify yourselves against tomorrow, and ye shall eat flesh: for ye have wept in the ears of the Lord, saying, who shall give us flesh to eat? For it was well with us in Egypt: therefore the Lord will give you flesh, and ye shall eat." Num.11: 16-18. "And Moses went out, and told the people the words of the Lord, and gathered the seventy men of the elders of the people, and set them round about the tabernacle. [25] And the Lord came down in a cloud, and spake unto him, and took of the spirit that was upon him, and gave it unto the seventy elders: and it came to pass, that, when the spirit rested upon them, they prophesied, and did not cease. [26] But there remained two of the men in the camp, the name of the one was Eldad, and the name of the other Medad: and the spirit rested upon them; and they were of them that were written, but went not out unto the tabernacle: and they prophesied in the camp. [27] And there ran a young man, and told Moses, and said, Eldad and Medad do prophesy in the camp. [28] And Joshua the son of Nun, the servant of Moses, one of his young men, answered and said, My Lord Moses, forbid them. [29] And Moses said unto him, Enviest thou for my sake? Would God that all the Lord's people were prophets, and

that the Lord would put his spirit upon them! [30] And Moses gat him into the camp, he and the elders of Israel." Numbers 11:24-30. "And in those days, when the number of the disciples was multiplied, there arose a murmuring of the Grecians against the Hebrews, because their widows were neglected in the daily ministration. [2] Then the twelve called the multitude of the disciples unto them, and said, It is not reason that we should leave the word of God, and serve tables. [3] Wherefore, brethren, look ye out among you seven men of honest report, full of the Holy Ghost and wisdom, whom we may appoint over this business. [4] But we will give ourselves continually to prayer, and to the ministry of the word. [5] And the saying pleased the whole multitude: and they chose Stephen, a man full of faith and of the Holy Ghost, and Philip, and Prochorus, and Nicanor, and Timon, and Parmenas, and Nicolas a proselyte of Antioch: [6] Whom they set before the apostles: and when they had prayed, they laid their hands on them." Acts 6:1-6

1. No war is ever won by a commandant.
2. A general without a company of soldiers is a defenseless officer.
3. If you have a manufacturing company. With a General Manager without operative staffs, you will not have production. The church like any other community need men and women who can channel her programs and defend her interest, even though you may have Pastors and preachers, the church cannot progress without a team of dedicated and committed workers.
4. The Pastor is not expected to do all the work alone –

   2 Tim.2: 1-2; Tit.1: 4-5.
5. God gave the Pastor and other ministerial gifts to the church to equip Christian to work Eph.4: 11-14.
6. Workers are needed to carry out designated assignment in the church and for the church Acts 6: 2-3.

7. Workers are needed because without them the work of God cannot progress Acts 6: 4-7.
8. The Pastor/leader does not possess all knowledge, God gave special abilities to different members of the church, for the benefit of all
Ex.35: 30-35; 36: 1-3.
9. God is not only looking for a crowd of followers but a team of works God wants disciples – Jn.8: 31.
10. God's vineyard is the whole world, all must work in the harvest of souls
Jn.4: 35-38.

WHO CAN WORK FOR GOD?

"Then said they unto him, What shall we do, that we might work the works of God? [29] Jesus answered and said unto them, this is the work of God, that ye believe on him whom he hath sent." John 6:28-29.

1. Those who are born-again Jn.3: 3; Lk.10: 17-20.

"Jesus answered and said unto him, Verily, verily, I say unto thee, Except a man be born again, he cannot see the kingdom of God." John 3:3

2. Those who have purged themselves

"Nevertheless the foundation of God standeth sure, having this seal, The Lord knoweth them that are his. And, Let everyone that nameth the name of Christ depart from iniquity. [20] But in a great house there are not only vessels of gold and of silver, but also of wood and of earth; and some to honor, and some to dishonor. [21] If a man therefore purge himself from these, he shall be a vessel unto honor, sanctified, and meet for the master's use, and prepared unto every good work." 2 Tim. 2:19-21

3. Those who are humble –Isa.57: 15.

"He hath shewed thee, O man, what is good; and what doth the Lord require of thee, but to do justly, and to love mercy, and to walk humbly with thy God?" Micah 6:8

4. Those who are teachable - A disciple is a learner
"Holding fast the faithful word as he hath been taught, that he may be able by sound doctrine both to exhort and to convince the gainsayers." Titus 1:9

5. Those who have given up self
And there went great multitudes with him: and he turned, and said unto them, [26] If any man come to me, and hate not his father, and mother, and wife, and children, and brethren, and sisters, yea, and his own life also, he cannot be my disciple. [27] And whosoever doth not bear his cross, and come after me, cannot be my disciple. [28] For which of you, intending to build a tower, sitteth not down first, and counteth the cost, whether he have sufficient to finish it? [29] Lest haply, after he hath laid the foundation, and is not able to finish it, all that behold it begin to mock him, [30] Saying, This man began to build, and was not able to finish. [31] Or what king, going to make war against another king, sitteth not down first, and consulteth whether he be able with ten thousand to meet him that cometh against him with twenty thousand? [32] Or else, while the other is yet a great way off, he sendeth an ambassage, and desireth conditions of peace. [33] So likewise, whosoever he be of you that forsaketh not all that he hath, he cannot be my disciple. Luke 14:25-33.

6. Those who are dependable 1 Kgs.20: 40.
"Moreover it is required in stewards, that a man be found faithful." *1 Cor.4: 2.*

7. Those who are Spirit filled –Acts 6: 5
"But truly I am full of power by the spirit of the Lord, and of judgment, and of might, to declare unto Jacob his transgression, and to Israel his sin." Micah 3:8.

LEADERS ARE TRAINED NOT BORN.

CHAPTER SIX

THE NEED FOR TRAINING

The work of God needs people but not just anybody. He needs those who have prepared themselves for leadership for example. Our Sunday school class especially that of children department, has been suffering in the hands of inexperienced teachers or leaders. It has been observed that the Pastor's vision in any local assembly is to get as many as possible into the church, but as the adults are coming in, they also come with their children.

The pastor will suddenly realize the need of separating the children from their parents because of disturbance. He will delegate the responsibility of taking care of the children to somebody in the church, who apparently is not equipped for such a responsibility and probably without the ability to endure the noise of the children. The parents are not disturbed but the children. The parents are not disturbed but the children's spiritual desires are not met. You can be sure the inexperienced teacher will keep them busy.

Our Pastors are trained and are well equipped in the Bible colleges or seminaries for at least two years. We as children teachers need to be well-trained for the work, not just sand wish a week seminar will be enough to handle the children. The fact is that leaders are trained not born. We can do better if we undertake a systematic training program that will equip us to reach the children for Christ. You can be more equipped and capable of leading the young ones to Christ than an evangelist or Pastor can do. Think about it! The Pastor might give a message about heaven for one hour and may not be able to get the message to little children, but the children teacher with a "Wordless Book" can explain heaven to a little child in fifteen minutes and the child will understand perfectly.

SEVEN REASONS FOR LEADERSHIP TRAINING

1. Leaders are trained so as to prepare them for leading
2. Leaders are trained so as to acquaint them with the technical and the methodology for successful leadership.
3. Leaders are trained to develop the God given ability that is residue within the individuals.
4. Leaders are trained to refresh ourselves and update our leadership skills.
5. Leaders are trained to transfer knowledge from one leader to another leader.
6. Leaders are trained to correct wrong conception of what leadership entails in the Christendom.
7. Leaders are trained to keep up the ministry of the church from one generation to the other generation.

A CASE STUDY

In 2 Samuel 18:21; 31-32; Joab had just killed Absalom the Son of David and wanted Cushi to go and tell the king what he saw.

"Then said Joab to Cushi, Go tell the king what thou hast seen. And Cushi bowed himself unto Joab, and ran." "And, behold, Cushi came; and Cushi said, Tidings, my lord the king: for the Lord hath avenged thee this day of all them that rose up against thee. [32] And the king said unto Cushi, Is the young man Absalom safe? And Cushi answered, The enemies of my lord the king, and all that rise against thee to do thee hurt, be as that young man is."

He did not teach him how to tell the king of the incident or what he should tell the king. He expected him to have known it. He went and did a wonderful job. He did not tell the king your son is dead but that all who hated the king should be as the young man. The king got the message and began to weep.

Now, look at another man, 2 Sam.18: 19-20, 22, 23-30.
"Then said Ahimaaz the son of Zadok, Let me now run, and bear the king tidings, how that the Lord hath avenged him of his enemies. [20] And Joab said unto him, Thou shalt not bear tidings this day, but thou shalt bear tidings another day: but this day thou shalt bear no tidings, because the king's son is dead." For all his judgments were before me: and as for his statutes, I did not depart from them. [24] I was also upright before him, and have kept myself from mine iniquity. [25] Therefore the Lord hath recompensed me according to my righteousness; according to my cleanness in his eyesight. [26] With the merciful thou wilt shew thyself merciful, and with the upright man thou wilt shew thyself upright. [27] With the pure thou wilt shew thyself pure; and with the froward thou wilt shew thyself unsavoury. [28] And the afflicted people thou wilt save: but thine eyes are upon the haughty, that thou mayest bring them down. [29] For thou art my lamp, O Lord: and the Lord will lighten my darkness. [30] For by thee I have run through a troop: by my God have I leaped over a wall."

He wanted to go and tell the king the progress at the war front.
Joab refused to send him to the ground that he was ignorant of what happened but he insisted he will go and share the information with the king.
He was called "Mr. Me – go" but he had no knowledge of what happened he eventually convinced Joab who permitted him to go but went and messed up before the king.
In the New Testament, we are told not to be novices – 1 Tim.3: 6. ***"Not a novice, lest being lifted up with pride he fall into the condemnation of the devil."***
God needs dedicated and well-equipped workers for His church. Are you that man or woman?

A person who has no vision only see what is immediate, what he can put his hands on, and what is convenient.

CHAPTER SEVEN

THE LEADER AND HIS VISION

"Where there is no vision, the people perish: but he that keepeth the law, happy is he." Proverbs 29:18. "Whereupon as I went to Damascus with authority and commission from the chief priests, [13] At midday, O king, I saw in the way a light from heaven, above the brightness of the sun, shining round about me and them which journeyed with me. [14] And when we were all fallen to the earth, I heard a voice speaking unto me, and saying in the Hebrew tongue, Saul, Saul, why persecutest thou me? it is hard for thee to kick against the pricks. [15] And I said, Who art thou, Lord? And he said, I am Jesus whom thou persecutest. [16] But rise, and stand upon thy feet: for I have appeared unto thee for this purpose, to make thee a minister and a witness both of these things which thou hast seen, and of those things in the which I will appear unto thee; [17] Delivering thee from the people, and from the Gentiles, unto whom now I send thee, [18] To open their eyes, and to turn them from darkness to light, and from the power of Satan unto God, that they may receive forgiveness of sins, and inheritance among them which are sanctified by faith that is in me. [19] Whereupon, O king Agrippa, I was not disobedient unto the heavenly vision: [20] But shewed first unto them of Damascus, and at Jerusalem, and throughout all the coasts of Judaea, and then to the Gentiles, that they should repent and turn to God, and do works meet for repentance. [21] For these causes the Jews caught me in the temple, and went about to kill me. [22] Having therefore obtained help of God, I continue unto this day, witnessing both to small and great, saying none other things than those which the prophets and Moses did say should come: [23] That Christ should suffer, and that he should be the first that should rise

from the dead, and should shew light unto the people, and to the Gentiles. [24] And as he thus spake for himself, Festus said with a loud voice, Paul, thou art beside thyself; much learning doth make thee mad. [25] But he said, I am not mad, most noble Festus; but speak forth the words of truth and soberness. [26] For the king knoweth of these things, before whom also I speak freely: for I am persuaded that none of these things are hidden from him; for this thing was not done in a corner. [27] King Agrippa, believest thou the prophets? I know that thou believest. [28] Then Agrippa said unto Paul, Almost thou persuadest me to be a Christian. [29] And Paul said, I would to God, that not only thou, but also all that hear me this day, were both almost, and altogether such as I am, except these bonds" Acts 26:12-29.

What is a vision? The dictionary defines vision as an act or faculty of seeing, thing, seen in a trance or dreams in imagination, state or period of such seeing, person or thing whose aspect transcends the natural.

Helen Keller was once asked, "What would be worse than being blind?" She replied, "To have sight with no vision." A person who has no vision only see what is immediate, what he can put his hands on, and what is convenient.

A MAN WITH A VISION

Alexander the Great had a vision. He conquered the known world. When he lost his vision, he couldn't conquer the liquor bottle.

When Noah had a vision, he could resist the mockery and built the ark that saved his household, when he lost the vision, he couldn't resist the liquor bottle.

When John Wesley had a vision, he moved out of the established tradition to preach Christ on horses back and founded the Methodist Church. When the early church had a vision, they went about preaching until they turn the world upside down.

WHAT TO DO WITH YOUR VISION?

The obvious answer is, you commit to act on the vision (That commitment is called a mission) and then design goals achieve the mission and thus fulfill the vision. That commitment includes a determination to overcome difficulties and eliminate obstacles.

A leader dishonors God when he professes a vision and then, when difficulties arise and enemies' assault, he complains, "God must not want this, or we would not be having so much trouble."

Instead, a leader is committed to his vision.

Leader used by God respond to the vision he gives them.

God gave Noah the vision of an ark, and he built it.

Abraham a city and he looked for it.

Nehemiah, a wall re-rebuilds.

Paul evangelizes the whole world.

David Living Stone a vision of Africa he opened the way for thousands of missionaries to preach the gospel.

John Sung the vision of evangelism in East Asia, and he changed the Spiritual complexion of every nation he visited.

If God has put a desire in your heart, accept the presence of the fulfillment of the vision. Failure to act on your vision can lead to personal stagnation, troubled Spirit, and a critical attitude. A God given vision is an awesome responsibility. Fulfillment can lead you to the heights of tremendous service to God and your fellow man. Failure to follow the vision will deprive others of the leadership they need.

The Christ – like leader needs to continually ask himself.

1. Will the vision produce results of beneficial permanence?
2. Will the vision move the people toward goals that fulfill their real needs?

For the Christ – like leader, a vision is a revelation of God's will. A leader grasps the challenge of the vision, commits to the mission, and implements the goals that will accomplish the mission and fulfill the vision.

But it all starts with a vision – the foundation of leadership.

GOALS

A vision is the foundation for all leadership. The leader's vision requires a commitment to act. That commitment is called a mission. But where the rubber meets the road is with a set of specific, measurable steps designed the achieve the mission. Those steps are called goals. A leader without goals is like a ship's captain without reference point or cross – country motorist without location signs and mileposts.

An effective leader must constantly sharpen the focus of his vision. He does this with effective goal setting. The clearer the leader's goals, the sharper his focus and vice-versa. Effective goal setting focuses the leader's vision by spelling out what steps he will take to accomplish that vision.

Henry Kaiser said, "Determine what you want more than anything else in life, write down the means by which you intend to attain it, and permit nothing to disturbed you from pursuing it."

Understand your mission.

Write down your goals.

List out your assets and a list of your liabilities.

Write down every quality or performance.

You could think of that indicated personal liability.

YOU MUST WRITE OUT YOUR GOALS

CHAPTER EIGHT

GOAL SETTING

"I will stand upon my watch, and set me upon the tower, and will watch to see what he will say unto me, and what I shall answer when I am reproved. [2] And the Lord answered me, and said, write the vision, and make it plain upon tables, that he may run that readeth it. [3] for the vision is yet for an appointed time, but at the end it shall speak, and not lie: though it tarry, wait for it; because it will surely come, it will not tarry" Habakkuk 2:1-3.

"Where there is no vision, the people perish: But he that keepeth the law, happy is he" Prov.29: 18.

What is your vision? Whatever it is, do you know how you will get there? Then you must write out your goal and each you must take, step by step. Leave no assumptions unstated. This will force you to analyze the resources you need – money, time, and personnel – and adjust your plan so that it is a realistic one that will reveals potential problem areas.

Setting goals simply involves writing out the steps it will take you to accomplish your vision. It may take five years, it may take twenty years, but the vision must be broken down into steps so that you know what you are to do to accomplish your vision, month-by-month, year-by-year. A good goal-setting should be S-M-A-R-T by that we mean it should be specific – Measurable – Attainable – Realistic – Tangible

1. **MAKE YOUR GOAL SPECIFIC:** Each goal must be specific step rather than a vague desire. You must describe the will move you toward the

accomplishment of your vision.

2. ***MAKE YOUR GOAL MEASUREABLE:*** *Goals should be measurable, not in terms of what is accomplished but when it was accomplished. Every goal should specify when the result would be achieved. The reason for this is that each goal is part of an entire goal system designed to fulfill your vision. Have a major goal and sub-goals.* ***"If you can't measure it, you can't monitor it."***

3. ***MAKE YOUR GOALS ATTAINABLE:*** *A man with a bass voice should not expect to become a soprano soloist. An illiterate should not expect to become a famous author within a period of three months. Don't waste your time trying to teach a horse to fly or a snake to sing* ***"The Halleluiah chorus."*** *- Set high goals, but not unattainable ones. Let the Holy Spirit guide you. Don't walk by sight. Believe the promises of God for your life* ***"With God all things are possible"*** *and with a believer* ***"Nothing shall be impossible"***

"And he said, the things which are impossible with men are possible with God" Luke 18:27.

"Jesus said unto him, If thou canst believe, all things are possible to him that believeth" Mark 9:23.

4. **MAKE YOUR GOALS REALISTIC:** State what result can be realistically achieved, given your available resources. Make provision for training and manpower development for member of your team and those who are to be involved in the actualization of your goals.

5. **MAKE YOUR GOAL TANGIBLE:** As you think about your goals, there will be some accomplishments that are intangible. You achieve these intangible goals by achieving related tangible ones. The goals you set before yourself should always be tangible.

CHAPTER NINE

PROGRAM PLANNING

"For which of you, intending to build a tower, sitteth not down first, and counteth the cost, whether he have sufficient to finish it? [29] Lest haply, after he hath laid the foundation, and is not able to finish it, all that behold it begin to mock him, [30] Saying, This man began to build, and was not able to finish. [31] Or what king, going to make war against another king, sitteth not down first, and consulteth whether he be able with ten thousand to meet him that cometh against him with twenty thousand? [32] Or else, while the other is yet a great way off, he sendeth an ambassage, and desireth conditions of peace" Luke 14:28-32. And they commanded the people, saying, When ye see the ark of the covenant of the Lord your God, and the priests the Levites bearing it, then ye shall remove from your place, and go after it. [4] Yet there shall be a space between you and it, about two thousand cubits by measure: come not near unto it, that ye may know the way by which ye must go: for ye have not passed this way heretofore. [5] And Joshua said unto the people, sanctify yourselves: for tomorrow the Lord will do wonders among you. [6] And Joshua spake unto the priests, saying, Take up the Ark of the Covenant, and pass over before the people. And they took up the Ark of the Covenant, and went before the people. [7] And the Lord said unto Joshua, This day will I begin to magnify thee in the sight of all Israel, that they may know that, as I was with Moses, so I will be with thee. [8] And thou shalt command the priests that bear the Ark of the Covenant, saying, When ye are come to the brink of the water of Jordan, ye shall stand still in Jordan. [9] And Joshua said unto the children of Israel, Come hither, and hear the words of the Lord your

God" Joshua 3:3-9.

Planning is an essential part of leadership and management PLOC – Planning – Leading – Organizing – Controlling. No war is won at the war front. ***"Failing to plan is planning to fail."*** Planning is success half gotten.

A leader must know how to plan for the successful implementation of his goals. Failure to plan is planning to fail.

Church planning is defined as making current decision in the light of the future expectations, which implies that the future may be different from the present. Special services such as Christmas, Easter and Thanksgiving are excellent opportunities to get new people in the church. These include special revival services and zonal crusades. A Pastor who does not have a vision to see his church grow will not see it grow. Hence the Pastor must structure his church for growth by careful planning of every phase of church activity.

Planning is not simply saying. This year we are going to have so many people added to our church. Planning relates to the whole disposition of the people. It relates to the spiritual levels within the church and to where God want you to go. Planning also corresponds to the faith level of the people.

Benefits of Planning

- Planning leads to efficiency.
- It helps to develop interesting programs that would help the members of the church.
- It leads to maximization of time, resources and materials.
- Planning reduces redundancy, tension complains, partisan spirit in the church.
- Planning is a powerful tool for church growth.
- Leads to fulfillment in the ministry.
- Helps in quick dissemination of information.

CHAPTER TEN

LEADERSHIP IS A CHOICE

You don't become a leader because you occupy a leadership position, your title don't make you a leader. You are a leader because you know the way, you can provide solution, and you see what others do not see. You are leader because you know the way and you can show the way to others and lead them to the way. You are a leader because you have a number of people that are following you, no matter how few. When you look behind you, you can see those persons your life had influence, people who are looking up to you as a model.

Those who consider you as a champion, some of them see you as their mentor. To be a leader, you must choose to lead, you must be conscious of leading, directing and guiding. Even if you have the call of God upon your life, you still must choose to become a leader. Whatever, your field, profession or vocation, you must make a decision to become a leader in that area, and with that purpose in mind you decide to come into leadership.

God created us with the ability to choose, you are created with a freewill, the power of choose.

> ***"I call heaven and earth to record this day against you, that I have set before you life and death, blessing and cursing: Therefore choose life, that both thou and thy seed may live." Deut.30: 19.***

God will not force you into leadership; you must be ready to accept the challenges and responsibilities of leadership. Choose to be a leader, be ready and willing to pay the price.

The place start is to be a good follower. You must submissive. Moses gladly transfer leadership to him, and God confirmed him as a leader of His people the children of Israel. Elisha followed Elijah, he received the mantle of leadership from him, when he got to the Jordan River, he relayed on the experience of what Elijah did before they cross the Jordan River. You need to learn under a leader, to be able to lead successfully. The place of training for leadership cannot be down play, if you must become a leader. Jesus had twelve disciples, they learnt from Him, they followed Him, and they did what He did. They knew His teachings and they were able to teach it. Daniel made up his mind to be different from others.

> ***"But Daniel purposed in his heart that he would not defile himself with the King's meat..." Dan.1: 8.***

If you must come to the front of others to lead the way, you must have some personal discipline; you have to sacrifice, so that you can come into excellent.

Are you ready for God, to use you and entrust you into leadership position. If yes, then you must be willing to pay the price for leadership. You must be willing to serve the people. Even though you are in front, but you are the servant. Leadership is service to the Lord and His people. A true leader is a person that choose serve others. Giving up your own convenes, giving up your sleep for others to sleep.

Leaders must be humble, even though they occupied exalted positions, yet they must exhibit humility. The way up is the way down. You must make a choice to be humble and keep being humble despite your status. Will you still want to accept the challenges of leadership? You must decide.

www.ingramcontent.com/pod-product-compliance
Lightning Source LLC
LaVergne TN
LVHW010123170826
845678LV00012B/2572

* 9 7 9 8 8 4 6 8 8 8 7 8 4 *